Insect or Spider?

How Do You Know?

Melissa Stewart

Enslow Elementary
an imprint of
Enslow Publishers, Inc.
40 Industrial Road
Box 398
Berkeley Heights, NJ 07922
USA

http://www.enslow.com

WHICH ANIMAL IS WHICH?

Contents

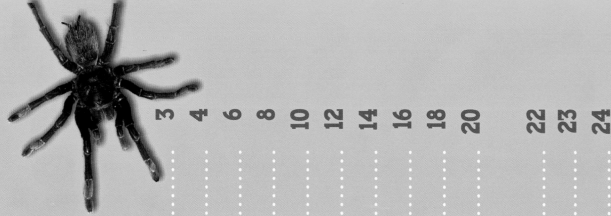

Words to Know

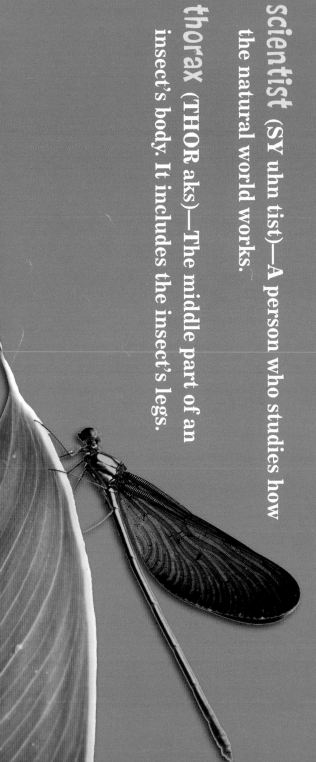

abdomen (AB duh min)—The back part of an insect's or spider's body.

antennae (an TEN ee)—The two long, thin body parts on the head of insects and some other animals. Antennae help animals sense the world around them.

cephalothorax (sef uh loh THOR aks)—The front part of a spider's body. It includes the spider's eyes, mouthparts, and legs.

scientist (SY uhn tist)—A person who studies how the natural world works.

thorax (THOR aks)—The middle part of an insect's body. It includes the insect's legs.

Do You Know?

Which of these animals is an insect? Which one is a spider? Do you know?

Three or Two Body Parts?

head

thorax

abdomen

Giant ant

An insect's body has three parts. The head is in the front. The thorax is in the middle. The abdomen is the part at the back.

A spider's body has two parts. The **cephalothorax** is in the front. It includes the spider's eyes, mouthparts, and legs. The back part of a spider's body is called the **abdomen**.

cephalothorax

abdomen

Wolf spider

Six Legs or Eight Legs?

German cockroach

An insect has six legs. A cockroach has long, thin legs for running.

A spider has eight legs. This spider uses its strong back legs to wrap insects in its web.

Black and yellow garden spider

Antennae or No Antennae?

An insect has two antennae on its head. It uses them to smell and touch the world.

Fire bug

Wolf spider

A spider does not have antennae. Scientists do not know how spiders smell things.

Wings or No Wings?

Most insects have wings. You can see this ladybug's wings because it is getting ready to fly.

Ladybug

Pink zebra tarantula

A spider
does not have
wings. It must
walk to get
around.

Two Eyes or Eight Eyes?

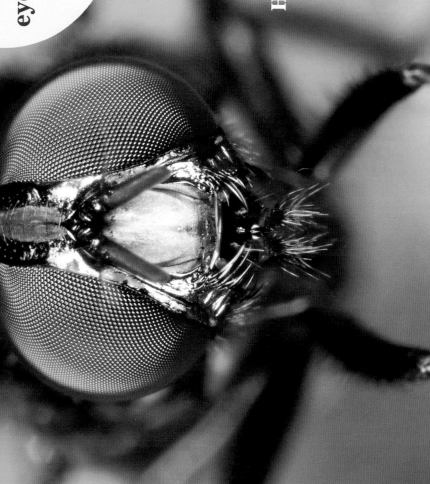

An insect has two large eyes. It can see very well.

House fly

Orange jumping spider

Most spiders have eight eyes. Some spiders see very well, but many do not. Their eyes can tell if it is light or dark. But they cannot see a clear picture of the world.

15

Veggies or Meat?

Insects eat many different kinds of foods. They may eat plants, dead animals, or even other insects. A few insects eat plastic, paper, or poop.

Bean leaf beetle

16

Crab spider catching a honey bee

Only one kind of spider eats plants. Most eat insects. Some spiders catch small frogs or mice.

How Do You Know?

It uses two antennae to smell and touch.

It sees with two large eyes.

Dragonfly

This animal has wings.

It has three body parts.

It has six legs.

It eats small flies and mosquitoes.

It's an insect!

It's a spider!

It has eight legs.

It has two body parts.

This animal does not have wings.

It eats insects.

Black and yellow garden spider

It does not have antennae.

It sees with eight simple eyes.

What a Surprise!

More than one million different kinds of insects live on Earth. Can you guess how many ants are alive right now? 10,000,000,000,000,000. That's a lot of ants!

Black ants

About 40,000 kinds of spiders live on Earth. Some spiders are tiny, but the Goliath spider is the size of a dinner plate.

Goliath bird-eating spider

21

Learn More

Books

Bishop. Nic. *Spiders.* New York: Scholastic, 2007.

Mound, Laurence. *Insect.* New York: DK Children, 2007.

Murawski, Darlyne A. *Spiders and Their Webs.* Washington, D.C.: National Geographic, 2004.

Walters, Martin. *The Illustrated World Encyclopedia of Insects.* London: Lorenz Books, 2009.

Web Sites

All About Insects
http://www.livescience.com/insects/

How Do Spiders Spin Their Webs
http://www.coolquiz.com/trivia/explain/
docs/spider.asp

Library of Congress Cataloging-in-Publication Data

Stewart, Melissa.
   Insect or spider? : how do you know? / Melissa Stewart.
      p. cm. — (Which animal is which?)
   Includes bibliographical references and index.
   Summary: "Explains to young readers how to tell the difference between insects and spiders"— Provided by publisher.
   Library Ed. ISBN 978-0-7660-3681-9
   Paperback ISBN 978-1-59845-237-2
   1. Insects—Juvenile literature. 2. Spiders—Juvenile literature. I. Title.
   QL467.2.S7767 2011
   595.7—dc22
                                                    2010003278

Printed in the United States of America

022013 Lake Book Manufacturing, Inc., Melrose Park, IL

10 9 8 7 6 5 4 3 2

To Our Readers: We have done our best to make sure all Internet Addresses in this book were active and appropriate when we went to press. However, the author and the publisher have no control over and assume no liability for the material available on those Internet sites or on other Web sites they may link to. Any comments or suggestions can be sent by e-mail to comments@enslow.com or to the address on the back cover.

♻ Enslow Publishers, Inc., is committed to printing our books on recycled paper. The paper in every book contains 10% to 30% post-consumer waste (PCW). The cover board on the outside of each book contains 100% PCW. Our goal is to do our part to help young people and the environment too!

Photo Credits: Photo Researchers, Inc.: Nigel Cattlin p. 8, Peter Menzel p. 21; © Scott Harms/ iStockphoto.com, p. 20; Shutterstock.com, pp. 1, 2, 3, 4, 5, 6, 7, 9, 10, 11, 12, 13, 14, 15, 16, 17, 18, 19, 23.

Cover Photos: Shutterstock.com.

Note to Parents and Teachers: The *Which Animal Is Which?* series supports the National Science Education Standards for K–4 science. The Words to Know section introduces subject-specific vocabulary words, including pronunciation and definitions. Early readers may need help with these new words.

Index